VICTORIAN STEAM

ROBIN JONES

PiXZ

First published in Great Britain in 2010

Copyright text and images, except where stated © 2010 Robin Jones/Diamond Head

British Library Cataloguing-in-Publication Data
A CIP record for this title is available from the British Library

ISBN 978 1 906887 89 6

PiXZ Books
Halsgrove House, Ryelands Industrial Estate,
Bagley Road, Wellington, Somerset TA21 9PZ
Tel: 01823 653777
Fax: 01823 216796
email: sales@halsgrove.com

An imprint of Halstar Ltd, part of the Halsgrove group of companies
Information on all Halsgrove titles is available at: www.halsgrove.com

Printed and bound in China by Toppan Leefung Printing Ltd

Introduction

The steam railway was the backbone of the Victorian age, the bridge link between the Industrial Revolution, the British Empire and the modern age.

In the companion Halsgrove volume *The Dawn of Steam*, we saw how Cornish mining engineers grafted steam technology on to the horse-drawn tramways, a concept which dated back centuries, to produce the first locomotives, and how 25 years later George and Robert Stephenson proved the success of steam haulage, by virtue of the victory of *Rocket* at the Rainhill Trials of 1829.

Rocket has been called the first 'modern' locomotive type. It marked a 'Big Bang' of locomotive development. As the Liverpool & Manchester Railway became the world's first inter-city line, it sparked a nationwide rush to link major centres of population with industrial heartlands and ports and harbours.

As railways evolved rapidly from being small local concerns serving mines and factories into main lines shrinking travelling times firstly throughout Britain and then the rest of the world, the scramble was on for locomotive engineers to produce more powerful, versatile and reliable locomotive types to suit every purpose, as outlined in *The Dawn of Steam*, which covers the period from the early 1800s to the middle of the century.

As the national rail network came together, rival companies competed to produce faster locomotives to claim a greater share of potential trade. There were the great Races to the North to see who could reach Scotland in the shortest time from London, which produced steam icons like Patrick Stirling's legendary Great Northern Railway 'singles.'

Elsewhere, smaller locomotives made a huge impact in industry, allowing sprawling private railway systems to serve colliery, ironmaking and quarrying complexes. The mid-19th century pioneering introduction of steam on lines like the Festiniog and Talyllyn railways opened up many new possibilities in the field of narrow gauge, hitherto the domain of horse traction.

By the end of the Victorian era, the earlier locomotives typified by gleaming brass steam domes, no cabs, huge stovepipe chimneys and enormous single driving wheels had given way to what we immediately recognised as 'modern' steam locomotive types — some of which were so successful that they lasted into the final decade of British Railways steam in the 1960s.

Not only that, but by the 1890s, steam locomotives were being built for tourism and leisure purposes, as evidenced by the Snowdon Mountain Railway and the Isle of Man's Groudle Glen Railway.

By process of evolution, the steam locomotive signalled its own downfall. Experiments with electric traction had gathered pace by the close of the century, and the Edwardian era marked the rise of the motor car and the invention of the first aircraft. Yet it is arguable that none of these would have happened if not for the invention of the self-propelled locomotive in the form of the steam engine, the invention that shrank the world and paved the way for the mass global communications of today.

To Vicky and Ross

1826

While locomotive manufacturers were locked in competition to produce new cutting-edge machines, many locomotives from the dawn of the steam age were still undertaking vital work in industry.

On display at Newcastle's Stephenson Locomotion Museum is the *Killingworth Billy*, built three years before *Rocket* for hauling wagons of coal to the staithes on the River Tyne. A development of Stephenson's earlier 'Killingworth Travelling Engine', some consider it to be the first commercially-successful form of locomotive.

It last ran under its own power in 1881 to mark the centenary of George Stephenson's birth, by which time it was all but 'Stone Age technology' having long been superseded by a plethora of magnificent machines as we will see in the pages that follow.

1848

Fire Queen was supplied new by marine engineers A. Horlock and Co in 1848 to run on the 4ft gauge Padarn Railway, which carried slate from the great Dinorwic Quarry in Caernarfonshire to the harbour of Port Dinorwic at Y Felinheli.

It was the first of the Welsh slate carrying lines to use steam locomotives. The Padarn Railway closed in 1961 and *Fire Queen*, a classic example of mid-19th century locomotive technology, is now a static exhibit in the National Trust's excellent Penrhyn Castle Railway Museum.

1864

Fletcher Jennings was an engineering company at Lowca near Whitehaven in Cumbria. It supplied the first and only two steam locomotives to run on the Talyllyn Railway in pre-preservation days. No 1 *Talyllyn*, an 0-4-2ST, is seen hauling a demonstration freight train at Fach Goch in 2008. The locomotive did not have a cab when delivered new in 1865 – one was added later – and it appears here in its original Victorian condition.

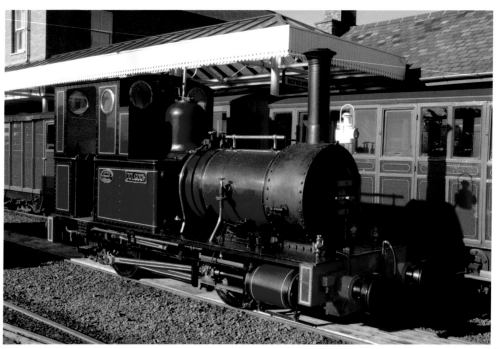

1866

Opposite: The Talyllyn Railway's No 2 *Dolgoch*, an 0-4-0 well tank, was built by Fletcher Jennings. It was the plight of this locomotive in 1949 that led to moves by West Midland enthusiasts to save this 2ft 3in gauge line in central Wales from closure, and in doing so became the first in the world to take over an existing railway on a voluntary basis.

Right: Midland Railway Class 156 2-4-0 tender locomotive No 158A was built at Derby in 1866 to a design by Locomotive Superintendent Matthew Kirtley for express passenger workings to London. A total of 29 members of the class were built.

The LMS recognised the significance of the type of which it inherited 21. No 156 was set aside for preservation — but was scrapped in 1932.

No 158A was rebuilt at various dates and was withdrawn at Nottingham in 1947 after ending its working days as station pilot. To make amends for the earlier scrapping, No 158A was preserved.

It appeared at the Stephenson Centenary Celebrations in Chesterfield in 1948 and was preserved at Derby Locomotive Works until moving to the Midland Railway-Butterley in 1975. It is part of the National Collection.

The only surviving locomotive from the world's first underground railway: Metropolitan Railway 4-4-0T No 23 was built by Beyer Peacock of Gorton in Manchester in 1866 and is one of the line's original A class locomotives used on the inner circle services until they were electrified in 1905.

Afterwards, it was switched to the longer suburban trains and was eventually relegated to the outpost of the Brill branch, where it worked until the line closed in 1935.

Afterwards, it was renumbered L45 and used on engineer's trains until 1948, when it had the distinctive of being the oldest working locomotive in Great Britain.

It was restored to as-built condition for the Underground centenary celebrations in 1963 and is now on display in London Transport Museum at Covent Garden.

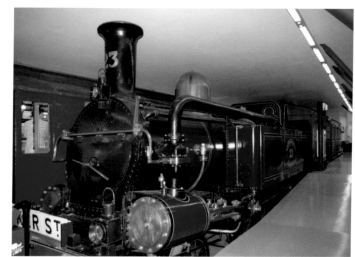

1869

North Eastern Railway Class X1 2-2-4T No 66 *Aerolite* was originally built in 1869 as a 2-2-2WT, as a replacement for an engine carrying the same name built by Kitson for the Great Exhibition of 1851 and which was destroyed in a crash in 1868. No 66 was rebuilt at Gateshead Works in 1892 as a 4-2-2T and rebuilt again as a 2-2-4T. It was used to pull inspection saloon trains. *Aerolite* was withdrawn in 1933 and preserved at the London & North Eastern Railway's York museum and can now be seen as a static exhibit at the city's National Railway Museum.

1870-1932

In 1870 the first of several different classes of four-wheeled saddle tank were supplied by the Hunslet Engine Company of Leeds to the narrow gauge slate quarry lines of North Wales, where they were a revelation. They became popularly known in enthusiast circles as 'Quarry Hunslets'. The majority of the locomotives that worked at the giant Dinorwic Quarry near Llanberis were eventually supplied by Hunslet. Several quarries had internal systems with lines serving different levels of the rockface.

A total of 52 were supplied between 1870 and 1932, including 29 by the end of the Victorian era. Many were used until the 1960s, when enthusiasts from both Britain and North America queued to buy them once they had been withdrawn.

Today, Quarry Hunslets can be found working at heritage railways throughout Britain. Ex-Penrhyn Railway locomotive *Lilian* (left, above), built in 1883, is now part of the Launceston Steam Railway fleet in Cornwall.

Left: After the Penrhyn Railway closed in 1962, 1893-built large Quarry Hunslet sisters *Blanche* and *Linda* (pictured at Porthmadog Harbour station) moved to the Ffestiniog Railway, where they were rebuilt as 2-4-0s and equipped with tenders.

Opposite: Former Dinorwic Quarry saddle tank *Cloister*, built in 1891, is now in regular service on the Amberley Museum line in Sussex.

1872

The Wotton Tramway, later Brill Tramway, had two Aveling & Porter 0-4-0 single-cylinder geared steam locomotives supplied in 1872, including No 1, now part of the London Transport Museum collection.

Looking more like traction engines than conventional railway engines, each of the 10-ton locomotives had a single overslung cylinder connected through a countershaft and pinion to further pinions on the axles. Their maximum speed was 8mph.

Both were later sold to Nether Heyford brickworks, near Weedon, Northamptonshire, which kept them until 1950.

The standard gauge line was built by the third Duke of Buckingham, who served as chairman of the London & North Western Railway from 1853-61. It ran from Quainton Road station to Brill.

Eventually, it became part of the London Transport portfolio, even though it was 51 miles from the heart of the capital, but was closed as early as 30 November 1935.

One of the most familiar classes of Victorian locomotives is the London, Brighton & South coast Railway A1 class 0-6-0Ts better known as 'Terriers'.

Designed by William Stroudley to haul commuter trains in south London, 50 were built between 1872 and 1880 at Brighton Works. Their nickname came about because of the distinctive 'bark' of the exhaust beat.

Fenchurch was preserved on the Bluebell Railway in 1964.

Douglas Earle Marsh, who succeeded Stroudley as Chief Mechanical Engineer of the LBSCR, reboilered 16 of them, and they became the A1X class. A total of 14 A1Xs and one A1 entered British Railways' service, their primary use being on the Kent & East Sussex Railway and the Hayling Island branch (where the train was nicknamed the Hayling Billy).

The unprofitable KESR closed in 1961 and the Hayling Island branch was axed the following year because of the condition of the bridge over Langstone Harbour. Withdrawn at the time the Hayling Island branch closed, No 32636 (formerly No 72 *Fenchurch*) was the oldest locomotive in British Railways' service. It moved to the Bluebell Railway for preservation in 1964, and was restored to its original identity. It is pictured working a demonstration goods train during a rare visit to the Isle of Wight Steam Railway.

Ten 'Terriers' are preserved, including No 82 *Boxhill*, a static exhibit at the National Railway Museum in York, and No 54 *Waddon* at the Canadian Railroad Historical Museum.

1875

When it arrived on the Bluebell Railway on 17 May 1960, LBSCR 'Terrier' No 55 *Stepney* became the first British Railways standard gauge locomotive to run on a heritage line. Rebuilt as an A1X in 1912, it was due for withdrawal in the 1920s, but instead was used on the Hayling Island branch, where it became BR No 32655.

The locomotive has been immortalised by appearing as itself in the Reverend Wilbert Awdry's Thomas the Tank Engine series of books, in its LBSCR golden ochre livery.

Stepney is seen heading a special VIP train at Kingscote to mark the 40th anniversary of the Bluebell Railway in 2000.

1876 *(top left)*

'Terrier' No 46 *Newington* was sold to the owners of a pub on Hayling Island named the Hayling Billy when it was withdrawn in 1963, and was displayed outside it for many years, before being donated in 1979 to the Isle of Wight Steam Railway, where, as W8 *Freshwater*, it is seen pulling a rake of the line's superbly-restored wooden-bodied coaches. The railway is also home to No 40 *Newport*.

1880 *(top right)*

The final operational A1X 'Terrier' in British Railway service was No 32678, which remained in service from Brighton shed until 10 August 1963. Originally numbered 78 and named *Knowle*, the 1880-built locomotive is seen at its Kent & East Sussex Railway home during a special 'Terrier' event in May 2006, which saw Bressingham Steam Museum's No 662 *Martello*, No 672 *Fenchurch* from the Bluebell Railway and *Stepney* reliveried as Brighton Works shunter No 32635, join home-based No 3 *Bodiam* for a reunion on the line they had all worked at some stage.

1873

Left: No 1 *Sutherland* was the first of 15 2-4-0Ts built by Beyer Peacock of Manchester for the 3ft gauge Isle of Man Railway. The design was adapted from a type the firm had supplied to the Cape Gauge sections of Norwegian State Railways.

Named after the Duke of Sutherland who was a director of the railway company, it was delivered in time for the official opening day on 1 July 1873. It remained in service until 1964 when it was withdrawn.

It briefly returned to service in 1998 for the Manx Steam 125 celebrations, using the boiler from No 8 *Fenella*, and even ran on parts of the Manx Electric Railway. No 1 is now stored at Douglas station.

Opposite: Teeside manufacturer Head Wrightson built 0-4-0 vertical-boilered tank engine No 33 'Coffee Pot' for use at Seaham Harbour, where it worked until 1962 as the 'dock' No 17. Its tiny proportions were perfect for working beneath the towering staithes on spilt coal reclamation and harbour breakwater maintenance work.

Preserved by Head Wrightson following withdrawal, in 1975 it was displayed at the Stockton & Darlington Railway 150th anniversary celebrations at Shildon. It is now on display at Beamish Museum in County Durham a world leader in the study of early railways.

Beamish has a similar but earlier Head Wrightson 'Coffee Pot', No 1, dating from 1871 when it was supplied to the Dorking Greystone Lime Company for use at its Betchworth quarry in Surrey. Last used there in 1949, Head Wrightson repurchased it in 1960. It returned to steam in March 2010 following its latest overhaul.

1874

Opposite: The first typical industrial saddle tank to be saved for preservation was Black Hawthorn 0-4-0 *Bauxite No 2*, which was set aside by ICI in 1947. This standard gauge shunter had been supplied new in 1874 for use at Hebburn Works, an aluminium smelting plant where it pushed wagons of bauxite rock into the smelters. It is said to be the Victorian equivalent of a forklift truck, typical of those used on internal industrial systems. Note its wooden buffers. It has never been repainted, and can now be seen in the Great Hall at the National Railway Museum in York.

Right: Looking every bit a classic piece of Victoriana is Haydock Foundry 0-6-0 well tank *Bellerophon*, part of the Vintage Carriages Trust collection.

It was built to serve the extensive internal standard gauge railway system at Haydock Collieries, Lancashire's biggest mining and engineering complex, and designed by owner Richard Evans' son Josiah. As well as running on the private system, it also hauled works outings over the main line to Blackpool.

It was withdrawn by the National Coal Board in 1964 and was donated to the Keighley & Museum Railway Preservation Society in 1966.

Bellerophon starred in the TV adaptation of Elizabeth Gaskell's *Cranford* at Christmas 2009, filmed on the Foxfield Railway where it went on loan. It is pictured hauling a Foxfield passenger train in December 2009.

Arguably the two greatest survivors from the Victorian age in operation today are the pair of London & South Western Railway 0298 class Beattie well tanks.

Designed by Joseph Beattie for London suburban services, the class was all but obsolete by the 1890s. However, because of their short wheelbase, a handful were shipped to Cornwall to work on the Wenfordbridge mineral line with its steep gradients and tight curves.

Several times they were earmarked for withdrawal and scrapping, but incredibly three of them lasted in service between Wadebridge, Bodmin and Wenfordbridge until 1962, because no newer locomotive type was deemed more suitable to handle the bends. They were finally replaced by GWR 1366 class pannier tanks.

No 30585 is preserved at the Buckinghamshire Railway Centre (pictured), while No 30587, part of the National Collection, is at the Bodmin & Wenford Railway, on 'home' territory.

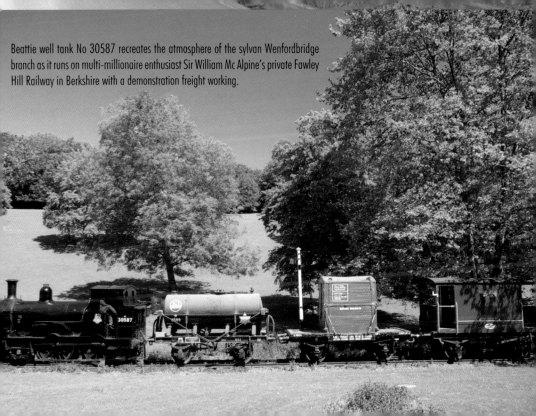

Beattie well tank No 30587 recreates the atmosphere of the sylvan Wenfordbridge branch as it runs on multi-millionaire enthusiast Sir William Mc Alpine's private Fawley Hill Railway in Berkshire with a demonstration freight working.

Built by the little-known Birmingham firm of Bellis & Seekings Ltd, 0-6-0 well tank *Secundus* was the second steam locomotive to work on the 2ft 8in gauge Furzebrook Tramway, one of the narrow gauge lines on the Isle of Purbeck heathlands serving ball clay pits and works. It worked until 1955 when most of the line was replaced by road transport, and was saved by the Birmingham Locomotive Club.

Secundus is now the star exhibit in the Swanage Railway's Corfe Castle station museum as a result of a loan agreement with Birmingham Museum.

1877

Built by de Winton of Caernarfon in 1877 for use in local slate quarries, vertical-boiled 0-4-0 *Chaloner* is one of the oldest narrow-gauge locomotives still in working order. In 1968, it became the first steam engine to run on the Leighton Buzzard Railway since 1921. It is seen here at the line's Page's Park headquarters, double-heading with Kerr Stuart 0-4-0ST *Peter Pan* of 1922 on a special train marking the 40th anniversary of the formation of what is now the Leighton Buzzard Narrow Gauge Railway Society on 9 June 2007.

In the restoration queue at Beamish Museum is one of only a handful of locomotives constructed by steamboat builder Stephen Lewin of Poole, Dorset. It was supplied to Seaham Harbour as an 0-4-0 well tank and became the system's No 18, and was converted on site to a saddle tank in 1936.

It was not withdrawn until 1969/70, and ran at Beamish for four years in the late seventies. No 18 is pictured at Seaham Harbour in its latter days there.

1879

This 0-4-0ST was built by Beyer Peacock for use as a shunter at its Gorton works in Manchester as No 1827. It was originally constructed as an 0-4-2ST with a crane mounted on the extended frames at the rear: the date at which the crane was removed is not known.

It is very similar to the later Lancashire & Yorkshire Railway 'Pug' 0-4-0STs — and their design is said by some to be based on No 1827. The locomotive was retired from shunting at Gorton and preserved in 1966. It is now based on the Foxfield Railway.

1880

Opposite: One of the most energetic of all surviving Victorian locomotives is Midland Railway 1377 class 0-6-0T No 41708, which was built at Derby to a Samuel Johnson design. Most of them, including No 41708 (original number 1708) were built with half-cabs, giving them their nickname 'Johnson half-cabs'. They were given the power classification 1F.

The first withdrawals came in 1928, and the last five remained in use until 1965, because of a contract signed by the Midland Railway in 1866 to provide shunting engines to Staveley Ironworks in Derbyshire for 100 years.

No 41708 was one of these Staveley engines, and in preservation has run on numerous heritage lines including the Midland Railway-Butterley, the Keighley & Worth Valley Railway the Swanage Railway and the Avon Valley Railway. It is now on static display at Barrow Hill roundhouse near Staveley, where it is pictured alongside LMS 'Black Five' No 45110.

Right: The North London Railway had 30 powerful goods locomotives built at Bow Works for freight traffic and shunting in the docks served by the line.

After the Grouping of 1923 when the NLR became part of the London, Midland & Scottish Railway, several of them including No 27505 were used on the steeply-graded Cromford & High Peak line in Derbyshire.

No 27505 was the last of the class and was withdrawn in 1960. It was obtained by the Bluebell Railway from Derby two years later.

It is seen on static display at the Ecclesbourne Valley Railway at Wirksworth in Derbyshire in 2005.

1882

London, Brighton & South Coast Railway Class B1 0-4-2 No 214 *Gladstone* was the first of a class of 36 designed by William Stroudley and built at Brighton Works. They comprised Stroudley's final express passenger design and while each was named after politicians, men associated with the railway, or places served by the LBSCR, the whole class became known as 'Gladstones'.

No 214 made history when it was withdrawn in 1927 and became the first main line locomotive to be privately preserved, by the Stephenson Locomotive Society. It is now on display in the Great Hall at the National Railway Museum in York.

1883

This 0-6-0 Kitson and Co. pannier tank was built to the Stephenson 'long boiler' design for the Consett Iron & Steel Company where it worked on the intensive internal system. It ended its working life at Derwenthaugh Coke Works. It is now a static exhibit at the North Tyneside Steam Railway.

1885

Still all but in its original condition, No 488 is the sole survivor of a class of 72 London & South Western Railway 4-4-2Ts known as the Adams radial tanks.

They were designed by William Adams for the LSWR's inner London suburban network, but were superseded by the M7s and displaced by third-rail electrification. The entire class was scrapped by 1927 apart from two kept for use on the Lyme Regis branch, where sharp curves made the use of other types of locomotive impossible. Many other classes were tried, but

they either couldn't cope with the heavy loaded holiday trains, or were too inflexible for the many curves.

No 488 had been sold to the military during World War One, and in 1919 was bought by the East Kent Railway. In 1946 it was bought by the Southern to add to the other two of the Lyme Regis branch, which they operated until 1960.

It was an early acquisition by the Bluebell Railway, chosen out of the three because it had an original Adams boiler – which now needs to be replaced before it can steam again. It is seen as Horsted Keynes in 1988, where the recreated stovepipe chimney completes the Victorian look.

1885

Opposite: The North Eastern Railway 1463 class of 20 2-4-0s (later LNER Class E5) were designed in 1884 for heavy express passenger work by a locomotive committee chaired by Henry Tennant. It was a superb design, and the engines proved they were capable of doing 40,000 miles per year, better than any other NER type.

Withdrawals took place between 1926 and 1929, but one, No 1463, was saved for posterity. It is on static display in Head of Steam, also known as Darlington Railway Centre & Museum.

Above: No 15 *Caledonia* is the only 0-6-0 on the Isle of Man Railway and the only steam locomotive not supplied by Beyer Peacock. It was Dübs & Co of Glasgow for the Manx Northern Railway, with the steep gradients of the Foxdale Railway in mind.

When the 3ft 6in gauge Snaefell Mountain Railway was being built, *Caledonia* was hired for works trains, tackling the 1-in-12 gradients after an extra rail was laid to accommodate it. *Caledonia* repeated its ascent of Snaefell during the line's centenary in 1995. It is pictured at Douglas station.

1886

In the 1880s, Potteries ironmasters Robert Heath & Sons were held to be the largest producers of bar iron in the world. Not only did the firm have its own private standard gauge network serving coal mines, forges furnaces and mills, but also built its own engines to run over it.

Robert Heath No 6 is the sole survivor of several 0-4-0STs whose design was all but copied at the firm's Black Bull base from one bought new from Falcon of Loughborough in 1885.

No 6 spent its working life at Black Bull and Norton collieries and, under National Coal Board ownership, received a new boiler in 1954.

The NCB donated it to Staffordshire County Council Museum for preservation and it moved to Shugborough Hall in February 1969. It was later exhibited at the now-closed Chatterley Whitfield Mining Museum before being bought by members of the Foxfield Railway who returned it to steam. It is pictured at Ludborough station while on loan to the Lincolnshire Wolds Railway in 2008.

1886

The unique Caledonian Railway 4-2-2 No 123, often known as the 'Caley single', was built to a design by Dugald Drummond by Neilson in Glasgow as a one-off exhibition locomotive, winning a gold medal at the Edinburgh International Exhibition in 1886.

It ran in regular traffic on the Carlisle to Edinburgh section of the West Coast Main Line.

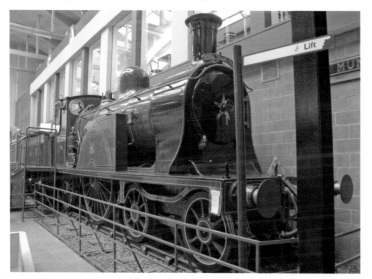

In the Races to the North against the East Coast Main Line trains to see who could reach Scotland from London soonest, No 123 often hit 56mph.

It became London Midland & Scottish Railway No 14010 at the Grouping of 1923 and ran express trains between Perth and Dundee.

Set aside for preservation after withdrawal in 1935, the engine is now a static exhibit in Glasgow Museum of Transport.

1887

North British Railway 0-4-0ST No 42 was built to the same design as *Kelton Fell*, and was one of the 38-strong G class (later Y9) used for shunting duties in ports and industrial sidings. In December 1962 it was the last of the class to be withdrawn, but was preserved at Lytham St Annes in Lancashire. It is now also on display in the Scottish Railway Exhibition at Bo'ness.

1887

Perhaps best known as The Green Dragon in the EMI big screen production of Edith A Nesbit's classic *The Railway Children*, Lancashire & Yorkshire Railway Class 25 0-6-0 tender locomotive No 957 designed by Chief Mechanical Engineer William Barton Wright. Built by Beyer Peacock in Manchester, the type became known as 'Ironclads'.

Withdrawn from British Railways' service as No 52044 in May 1959, it became one of the earliest private locomotive preservation schemes when it was bought by Tony Cox, who later became secretary of the Worth Valley Railway Preservation Society. He brought it to the Keighley & Worth Valley Railway in March 1965 and after extensive rebuilding it is now part of the operational fleet.

1889 *(top right)*

The Lancashire & Yorkshire Railway Class 5 2-4-2Ts (the 'Lanky tanks') were introduced by Chief Mechanical Engineer John Aspinall as a replacement for the 0-4-4Ts.

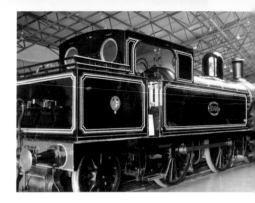

1891 *(lower right)*

The North Eastern Railway Class C (later J21) 0-6-0 tender engine as designed by Locomotive Superintendent Thomas William Worsdell was a workhorse in the truest sense of the word. In short, it made the coalfields and industrial areas of the north east tick.

Originally built for mineral trains, later they saw widespread use on passenger and mixed traffic duties. They operated the intensive passenger service on the Newcastle to South Shields route until electrification in 1938.

No 65033 was the last J21 to work for British Railways, taken out of service in April 1962. Luckily, it stood at Darlington for five years without attracting a scrapman's attention. In 1967, it was saved for the then-embryonic Beamish Museum.

It is now at the North Norfolk Railway under the custodianship

of a new group, the Locomotive And Conservation Learning Trust, which is seeking to raise £500,000 to rebuild it to running order, as a 'People's Engine' representing ordinary workaday locomotive types. Further details on the appeal may be found at www.lclt.org.uk

1891

London & South Western Railway O2 0-4-4T W24 *Calbourne* is synonymous with steam on the Isle of Wight.

One of a class which once numbered 60, it was built at Nine Elms Works to a design by Chief Mechanical Engineer William Adams. First allocated to Fratton and Exeter, in 1925 the Southern Railway sent it to the Isle of Wight as part of a major upgrade of the island's railway network. A total of 23 O2s ended up on Wight and by 1960 were the only class of steam engine operating there.

Following the wholesale closures of the 1950s and '60s, only the Ryde Pier Head to Shanklin route was saved, and was electrified in early 1967 to take redundant London Underground tube stock. *Calbourne* was used on engineers' works trains on this line before it was sold to the Wight Locomotive Society, which set up today's Isle of Wight Steam Railway.

In the 1990s, it was returned to its early 1930s condition, with Southern Railway olive green livery and an unmodified coal bunker.

1891

Another big star of EMI's *The Railway Children* was Manning Wardle 0-6-0ST *Sir Berkeley*. Supplied new to engineering contractors Logan & Hemingway, it was used on many railway construction projects including the Manchester, Sheffield & Lincolnshire Railway, later the Great Central.

It was sold to the Cranford Ironstone Company of Kettering in 1935 where it received the nameplates *Sir Berkeley* from a scrapped Manning Wardle engine. Retired from service at nearby Byfield Quarries in 1963, it was bought a year later by enthusiast Roger Crombleholme, who took it to the Keighley & Worth Valley Railway. Current owner the Vintage Carriages Trust has loaned it to the Middleton Railway near Leeds.

1891

North Eastern Railway locomotive superintendent Thomas W. Worsdell, had the first six H (later Y7) class 0-4-0Ts built in 1888. Their short wheelbase easily tackled the tight curves and poor quality track of dock lines and freight lines and sidings on which they ran. They were initially allocated to Tyneside, at Hull Docks, and within Darlington Works.

A further ten were ordered in 1891, and No 1310, which in 1965 passed into the ownership of the Steam Power Trust and is based at the Middleton Railway near Leeds, was among them. By 1923, 24 had been constructed, including 1923-built No 68088, which has also been preserved.

1891

Well remembered as the '*Play School* engine', *Swanscombe* is the oldest surviving Barclay locomotive in the United Kingdom.

The 0-4-0ST was delivered new to the Northfleet Coal and Ballast Co. Kent, and later moved to West Thurrock in Essex to run on quarries and wharves. Passing into the ownership of the Thurrock Chalk and Whiting Company, later part of the Blue Circle Group, it was bought for preservation in 1965 and moved to what is now the Buckinghamshire Railway Centre at Quainton Road in 1969. It was resteamed in 1975 for BBC TV's *Play School* and has since been driven by the Duke of Gloucester and featured in an episode of *Midsomer Murders*. Its latest relaunch following overhaul came in 2010.

1891

Robert Stephenson & Co built 0-6-0T *Twizell* for industrial service in County Durham. Part of the Beamish Museum collection, it is on loan to the Tanfield Railway. Named after a local burn (stream), Robert Stephenson 0-6-0 tank engine *Twizell* was preserved by Beamish Museum out of National Coal Board service in 1972. In March 2010 it steamed again on the nearby Tanfield Railway following an extensive overhaul.

1893

The 20 London & South Western Railway LSWR T3 class express passenger 4-4-0s were designed by William Adams.

Withdrawals started in 1930, and the last, No 563 was set aside for preservation in August 1945. It is now on static display in Locomotion: The National Railway Museum at Shildon.

1893

National Railway Museum exhibit No 790 *Hardwicke* is the last of the London & North Western Railway Improved Precedent or 'Jumbo' class of 166 2-4-0s designed by Francis Webb for express passenger use and built at Crewe Works.

On 22 August 1895, Hardwicke took two hours and six minutes for the 141-mile run from Crewe to Carlisle, with an average speed of 67.1 mph, establishing a new speed record during the 'Race to the North.'

Withdrawals started as early as 1905, the last in service, No 5001 *Snowdon*, taken out of traffic in 1934. *Hardwicke* was withdrawn in 1932 and preserved, later becoming part of the National Collection. Returned to working order in 1976, it hauled some main line excursions. It is currently a static exhibit.

1893

Wilson Worsdell's first express passenger locomotives for the North Eastern Railway were the Class M1 4-4-0s. They were used on the East Coast Main Line, including the York to Edinburgh stretch of the then newly-introduced 2.30pm dining trains. They were heavily used during the 1895 'Race to Aberdeen'.

The London & North Eastern Railway reclassified them as D17. The first D17 to be withdrawn was No 1628 following a collision at Hull Paragon station in 1927, but regular withdrawals began four years later. The last two were withdrawn in 1945, No 1629 being scrapped but No 1621 saved for York Railway Museum, later superseded by today's National Railway Museum where it is on static display.

1893

The London & South Western Railway's Locomotive Superintendent William Adams designed the B4 class of 25 0-4-0T dock tanks for shunting in locations with sharp curves. They were built at Nine Elms works.

Two survive: No 96 *Normandy* (pictured) at the Bluebell Railway and No 102 *Granville* at Bressingham Steam Museum near Diss in Norfolk.

1894

The Manchester firm of Sharp Stewart & Co delivered 15 locomotives to the Highland Railway to a revolutionary design by locomotive superintendent David Jones in 1894. Based on US practice, they were the first 4-6-0s to run in the British Isles and when unveiled, they were the most powerful main line engines in the country. Intended as freight engines, they were often pressed into passenger service.

While the class brought widespread acclaim for Jones, he was badly scalded while testing one and eventually retired due to ill heath.

The London Midland & Scottish

Railway earmarked No 103 for preservation in 1934. It was returned to running order by British Railways in 1959 and between then and 1966, hauled many enthusiast specials and appeared in the film *Those Magnificent Men in Their Flying Machines*. The only surviving Highland Railway locomotive, it is now a static exhibit in the Glasgow Museum of Transport.

1894

Left: Between 1891 and 1902, the Great Eastern Railway built 100 T26 (later E4) class mixed traffic 2-4-0s to a design by James Holden and they could be seen throughout East Anglia. They were intended to haul the increasing agricultural traffic and cross-country and slow main line passenger services.

The class were heavily involved with the movement of horses by rail to and from Newmarket racecourse, and so could be seen at work far outside the GER system. They were also used on passenger trains to the Norfolk coast, particularly Wells-next-the-Sea and Cromer.

British Railways inherited 18 of them at nationalisation. The last to be withdrawn, in 1959, was No 490 (BR No 62785) which became part of the National Collection and is on static display at Bressingham Steam Museum.

Opposite: **1894** By late Victorian times, it was realised that railways had developed an enthusiast following, and Sir Arthur Heywood pioneered attempts to build miniature versions of what was happening on the main line. His 15in gauge passenger-carrying Duffield Bank Railway was built in the grounds of his house on the hillside overlooking Duffield in Derbyshire in 1874, and he later built the Eaton Hall Railway for the Duke of Westminster.

His work inspired the great model builder Wenman Joseph Bassett-Lowke who began developing miniature railways on a commercial basis in the 20th century. In 1915, Bassett-Lowke and his friend R. Proctor-Mitchell bought the derelict 3ft gauge Ravenglass & Eskdale Railway and relaid it to 15in gauge. When Heywood died in 1916, the locomotives and rolling stock from Duffield Bank line were acquired, including *Muriel*, which dated from 1894, and whose frames and running gear were rebuilt as 0-8-2 *River Irt*. The locomotive is still in regular service today.

1895

Snowdon Mountain Railway 0-4-2T No 2 *Enid*, named after Enid Assheton-Smith, who cut the first sod when construction of the line started in 1894, passes Clogwyn en route to the roof of Wales. The 2ft 7½in gauge line, Britain's only rack railway which opened in 1896, used steam locomotives supplied by SLM of Winterthur in Switzerland. Their boilers, cab and general superstructure are tilted forward at an angle because of the line's steep gradient. Steam engines can operate only when the boiler is level, because it needs water to cover the boiler tubes and firebox sheets at all times. These locomotives cannot function on level track, and so the whole railway, including sheds and workshops, must be laid on a gradient.

1896

No 4 *Snowdon* is pictured at the Snowdon Mountain Railway's Llanberis base station. The railway is built with a central rack rail; pinions on the locomotive driving wheels are constantly engaged with the rack, and apart from providing adhesion, powerful brakes which grip the rack rail solidly can be immediately applied. The fact that these engines are still doing exactly the work they were designed for, carrying tourists to the top of Snowdon, is a tribute both to both their builders and the caring maintenance that has been lavished on them ever since.

1896

The Bluebell Railway is home to the only remaining South Eastern & Chatham Railway O1 class 0-6-0 tender locomotive.

Built at Ashford Works, the O class, as the type was originally known, were the main freight engines of the South Eastern Railway until it merged with the London, Chatham & Dover Railway in 1899. Afterwards, they were displaced by the more powerful C1 class 0-6-0s, and relegated to branch line duties including passenger trains. They were to be seen in regular use on the Kent & East Sussex and East Kent railways.

The last members of the class had been withdrawn by British Railways 1962, but No 65 survived, even though the scrapman had begun cutting it up. It became part of the short-lived Ashford Steam Centre project before it was moved to the Bluebell Railway where it was returned to steam in time for the centenary of the amalgamation of the SER and LCDR in 1999. It was turned out in SECR goods livery, matching Bluebell stablemate livery carried by C class No 592, which was built in 1902. The pair are pictured double heading during the event, with No 65 leading.

1896

John Aspinall's Lancashire & Yorkshire Railway Class 27 0-6-0s were the company's standard goods engine and 484 were built between 1889-1918 at Horwich Works. They were so successful that around 50 were still in British Railways' service as late as the summer of 1960. One of them, No 1300, survived into preservation on the East Lancashire Railway.

1896

The 2ft gauge Groudle Glen Railway, which runs for three-quarters of a mile from Lhen Coan, a point near the Manx Electric Railway's Groudle Hotel stop through the glen to Sea Lion Rocks, where they was a zoo, opened on 23 May 1896, with a Bagnall 2-4-0T called *Sea Lion* heading the trains. A second, *Polar Bear*, followed in 1905.

The line closed in 1962, but was rebuilt by the Isle of Man Steam Railway Supporters' Association and officially reopened on 23 May 1986 as part of Manx Heritage Year. *Sea Lion* returned permanently in September 1987.

1897

The Great Western Railway's famous Dean Goods or 2301 class of 0-6-0 tender locomotives appeared in 1893 and continued in production for another six years at Swindon Works to the design of William Dean. They were a radical departure from previous GWR types because they had inside frames only.

The type saw service on the continent during both world wars: after several were abandoned in France following the retreat to Dunkirk in 1940s, many were used by the Nazi occupying forces. At least two ended up behind the Iron Curtain. The last in service on British Railways was No 2538 which was withdrawn in May 1957.

No 2516, built in 1897, is the sole survivor of a class of 280, and is currently a static exhibit at STEAM: Museum of the Great Western Railway, which occupies part of Brunel's Swindon Works.

The M7 0-4-4Ts were the first new class of locomotive introduced by Dugald Drummond after he became Locomotive Superintendent of the London & South Western railway in 1895. The first appeared in 1897 and construction continued in batches until 1911, with five significant design variations. A total of 105 were built and they gave sterling service. Initially, some of them worked semi-fast passenger services between London and Portsmouth, Bournemouth and Weymouth and Exeter and Plymouth, but following a high-speed derailment near Tavistock in 1898, they were used on local main line and branch workings along with London suburban services.

The class was gradually replaced from the 1950s onwards, firstly by new lightweight standard steam classes and then diesels and electric locomotives. By the end of 1963, most of the survivors were shedded at Bournemouth to work the Swanage branch.

Two survived into preservation, 1897-built No. 245, which remained in service until 1962, as a static exhibit at the National Railway Museum in York, carrying its original LSWR livery, and 1905-built No 30053, which was sold to the Steamtown museum in Bellows Falls, Vermont, USA 1967, but was repatriated in 1987 and now runs on the Swanage Railway.

Bagnall 0-4-0ST No 1491 *Isabel* was built for the 2ft gauge Cliffe Hill Mineral Railway which linked Cliffe Hill granite quarry to the London Midland & Scottish Railway between Leicester and Coalville, and which operated from 1896 until 1948. *Isabel* is now preserved at the Amerton Railway at Stowe-by-Charley in Staffordshire.

1898

By the mid-1890s, the Great Northern Railway realised that its passenger locomotives were outdated. The Stirling single-wheelers of the day could not match the faster speeds and heavier loads seen on rival companies.

In 1895, the board appointed Henry Alfred Ivatt as Chief Locomotive Superintendent to replace Stirling, and he looked towards the Atlantic 4-4-2 wheel arrangement by then commonplace in the USA.

He was authorised to build an experimental 4-4-2 in February 1897, and a year later No 990 was completed. The first 4-4-2 built in Britain, it was nicknamed 'Klondike' after the 1896 Yukon gold rush. In June 1900, No 990 was named *Henry Oakley*, and altogether a total of 22 'Klondikes' were built.

The first was withdrawn in 1935, five soldiering on during World War Two.

Henry Oakley was preserved in 1937 and sent to York Railway Museum. It returned to the main line in 1953, running specials to mark the Doncaster Works centenary.

Part of the National Collection, it is now on static display at Bressingham Steam Museum.

SOUTHERN
B
473

1898

Opposite: The London, Brighton and South Coast Railway E4 class 0-6-2Ts designed by Robert Billinton for local passenger, freight and branch line duties and built by Brighton Works gave stalwart service until the mid 1950s when they began to be replaced by multiple units, or declared surplus to requirements because of line closures. The last was withdrawn in 1964.

No 32473 (LBSCR No 473 *Birch Grove*) was one of the last survivors and was bought in 1963 for use on the Bluebell Railway. After its most recent overhaul it returned to traffic on January 2010 in 1920s Southern Railway green.

Right: No 1338 is the sole surviving locomotive from the Cardiff Railway, which was owned by the Marquis of Bute and at just 11 miles was the smallest line absorbed into the Great Western at the Grouping of 1923. It ended its day working at Swansea Docks and was withdrawn by British railways in 1963.

It was preserved at the long-vanished Bleadon & Uphill station museum in Somerset in April 1964, and after arriving at Didcot Railway Centre in 1987, it was restored to working order. It is seen in action alongside a steam lorry at a Bristol Harbour Railway photo charter in 2000.

1898

Steam still runs on part of the Metropolitan Railway, in the form of the company's E class 0-4-4T No 1.

It is only survivor of a class of seven engines designed by the Chief Mechanical Engineer of the Met, T. F. Clark, for use on the Baker Street to Verney Junction service. It was also the last locomotive constructed at Neasden Works.

No 1 worked the last steam train on the Chesham Branch in July 1960 and the last steam-hauled passenger train anywhere on London Transport in 1961.

As L44, it was withdrawn two years later after taking part in the Metropolitan Centenary parade at Neasden on 23 May 1963, where it hauled four bogie coaches and a milk van.

Afterwards, it was bought by the London Railway Preservation Society and delivered in steam on 26 March 1964 to the group's temporary store at Skimpot Lane, Luton.

It is now part of the operational fleet at Buckinghamshire Railway Centre at Quainton Road station, once a northern outpost of the Met.

1899

Top left: Great Northern Railway J13 0-6-0ST, classified J52 by the London & North Eastern Railway, is the sole survivor of a class designed by Henry Ivatt and introduced in 1897, based on the earlier domeless J14 class. A total of 85 J13s were built up to 1909, while several J14s were rebuilt as J13s from 1922.

No 1247, by then renumbered 68846, was bought by Captain Bill Smith in 1959 and became the first British Railways locomotive to be privately preserved. In 1980 it was donated to the National Railway Museum and is now on static display in Locomotion: The National Railway Museum at Shildon.

Bottom left: Based at the Strathspey Railway in the Highlands is Caledonian Railway 812 class 0-6-0 No 828, the last of 96 designed by John F. McIntosh for express goods trains, excursion traffic and the Clyde Coast fast boat trains connecting with the company's steamers.

Seventeen were fitted with Westinghouse air brakes for passenger train working, including No 828, which was built at St Rollox works.

The class was so successful that the last examples were withdrawn from traffic in 1963.

No 828 is the only locomotive of pure McIntosh design remaining in Britain and is therefore unique.

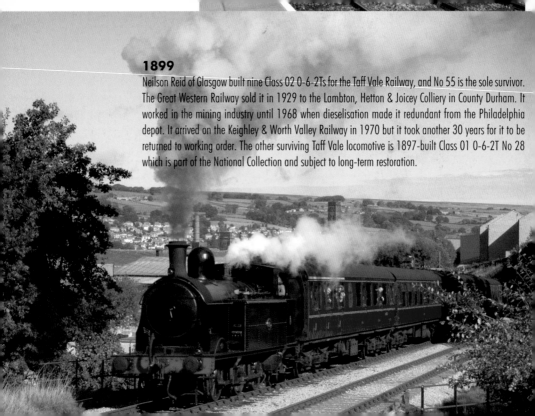

1899

Neilson Reid of Glasgow built nine Class O2 0-6-2Ts for the Taff Vale Railway, and No 55 is the sole survivor. The Great Western Railway sold it in 1929 to the Lambton, Hetton & Joicey Colliery in County Durham. It worked in the mining industry until 1968 when dieselisation made it redundant from the Philadelphia depot. It arrived on the Keighley & Worth Valley Railway in 1970 but it took another 30 years for it to be returned to working order. The other surviving Taff Vale locomotive is 1897-built Class O1 0-6-2T No 28 which is part of the National Collection and subject to long-term restoration.

1901

Between 1891 and 1910, the Lancashire & Yorkshire Railway built a class of 57 0-4-0STs for shunting sharply curved sidings in the industrial areas and docks of Fleetwood, Goole, Liverpool and Salford.

They were affectionately known as 'Pugs' and under the London Midland & Scottish Railway, they were allocated to sheds as far away as Bristol, Bangor, Crewe, Derby, Widnes, York and Swansea. British Railways withdrew the last one in 1963.

No 51218 is the elder of the two survivors. Originally L&Y No 68, it was preserved in 1965 and is based on the Keighley & Worth Valley Railway. The Lancashire & Yorkshire Railway Society also owns No 19, which was built in 1910.

1898

Dugald Drummond designed his London & South Western Railway T9 4-4-0s for express passenger work in south west England, with a total of 66 built.

They were popular with their crews who nicknamed them 'Greyhounds' because of the excellent turn of speed expresses. They were extremely effective west of Salisbury where their light axle loadings and short frame lengths adapted well to the tight curves of the Southern's Western Section.

Following the replacement of steam by diesels on the routes they worked, all were withdrawn by 1961. No 120 (BR No 30120), was saved for preservation as part of the National Collection. It was repaired at Eastleigh Works and returned to service in LSWR green for special trains in 1962.

Following an appeal by *Heritage Railway* magazine, it has found a new home at the Bodmin & Wenford Railway, where it returned to running order in 2101 following an overhaul.

Picture credits

All pictures by the author apart from the following to whom grateful thanks are due:

Alex Eyres/Talyllyn Railway: 7; Amberley Museum: 13; Buckinghamshire Railway Centre: 42, 60; Ecclesbourne Valley Railway: 29; Ffestiniog Railway: 12; Foxfield Railway: 21; Richard Holland/Steam Power Trust: 41; Isle of Wight Steam Railway: 17, 39; Paul Jarman/Beamish Museum: 26, 31, 43, 62; Launceston Steam Railway: 12; Lancashire & Yorkshire Railway Trust: 37; Leighton Buzzard Railway: 25; Lincolnshire Wolds Railway: 34; London Transport Museum: 14; Isle of Man Railways: 18, 33; Penrhyn Castle Railway Museum: 6; Brian Sharpe: 9, 35, 38, 47, 48; Geoff Silcock: 17; Snowdon Mountain Railway: 40, 41; Stephenson Locomotive Museum: 5; Colin Tyson: 58; Vintage Carriage Trust: 40; Andrew PM Wright/Swanage Railway: 24; Paul Jarman/Beamish Museum: 1889 J21: 38; Anthony Coulls/Locomotion: 1983 T3: 43; Brian Sharpe: 1899 Taff Vale 55: 62.